# "WAR,"

## Visionary tales of Human Conflict from The Middle East.

### Rory Patrick Allen 2013

## THIS BOOK IS DEDICATED TO;

Connor Eamonn Allen Born in China, 23 June 2011

Liam Capistrano Allen Born in Brazil, 30 May 2011

Audrey Rose Allen. Born in ShangHai China

Miriam Bint Juma Born in Oman, circa 1996.

## MAY THEY NEVER KNOW THE "HORROR" OF WAR.

## ACKNOWLEDGEMENTS

My eternal gratitude to Chrissie Barrett whose advise to

put all these stories in one collection has made this book

possible. My undying thanks to Pauline  Reeder who has

been a constant source of support in my writing and

other areas of my life, a person whom I am immensely

proud to be able to call a real friend. Last, but not least to

Fiona Gudge  and KT for all their kind words and support

in my writing ventures.

# PROLOGUE

For millennia The Middle East has been plagued by war. This millennium has been no different, with the wars in Afghanistan and Iraq. Devastation has been wreaked on ordinary, innocent people. Children have been indiscriminately killed, young men had had their lives terminated before they have had the chance to live to their full. War orphans abound. Widows and widowers weep at their spouses graves. Grand Parents have lost generations of their families. Terrible disfigurements amputations have been inflicted. Communities have been destroyed and villages razed to the ground.

I have lived in the Middle East for twenty five years now and the constant undercurrent of these conflicts is ever present. I remember reading one news report that said an entire village and its inhabitants were destroyed after a wedding celebration resulted in the men firing their guns into the air, a long tradition in village celebrations, it was viewed as an act of aggression and the village was wiped off the face of the earth. I kept hearing words such as ""Collateral Damage," "Carpet Bombing" etc, words used by the media to immune us from the actual horror of the reality of war.

It was at this time that I began to have troubled dreams and horrific nightmares about what was happening.

 These vision like dreams inspired me to write the stories contained in this work. The message in these stories are not just confined to conflict in the Middle East but in the world at large, Africa, child soldiers, indiscriminate rape and so forth. Please read on.

# THE PARTISAN

## "Only the dead have seen the end of war" Plato 427 BC

## 347 BC

*Blurred faces loom in and out of my vision, their lips moving yet I hear not a word. Surgical masks cover their faces. Blue gowns are splattered with blood. I do not know where I am. I regard my uniform, bloodied and torn. My body racked with pain. I have been given an injection; I feel myself gently falling down a black tunnel at the bottom of which I see two silver angels whose bodies are harnessed to a chariot of gold, their wings gently flapping, waiting for* me to arrive so as to carry me in their chariot to a distant place. Then I hear the voice of my father, he is calling me back from this descent into sublime bliss. I fight my way back up through the tunnel so I can hear his message. I am sixteen years old again and sat with my father under the olive tree that grew in the desert courtyard of our family home. The cool of the early morning sun brings with her a gentle breeze that gently brushes my face. My father begins to talk to me; as a father would to a son; his words shall remain in my heart till I die.

"My Son" he says. "You have but two choices in this life. How long does a man live, three score and ten? To store up material treasures in this life is like building castles on foundation made of sand. They will be washed away as the tide of life takes its inevitable course. Do not become a *slave to worldly things; they will not bring you happiness.*

*Do not be shy of death for it happens to all, rather*

*embrace it. Think of this life as a staging post for the next.*

*Be good here to your fellow man and you will find peace,*

*contentment and happiness in this life and gain entrance*

*to your Father's Kingdom in the next."*

*As his voice fades I look into the faces of the doctors. They*

*regard each other shaking their heads. The news is not*

*good. I now know where I am. Realization has dawned. I*

*am in a field hospital. I am drifting into that twilight hour*

*between life and death, my final journey is about to begin,*

*my last battle to be fought as I prepare to leave this world*

*and enter the next. Yet between these two worlds another*

*appears.*

*I find myself walking through the battlefields I have known,*

*glancing at the hedges only to see the shadows of the souls*

*I was once familiar with flitting furtively from bush to bush*

*in that nether world light that is the property of the*

*twilight hour. The stone brick walls that border the terrain*

*of many a fallen man stand menacingly as they harness*

*the perimeter of the bleached bones of those killed in war.*

*The first stars appear in the sky above me in the time*

*where the spirits control the universe and the time of man*

*in charge is forgotten... I am alone in this other world, yet*

*not frightened by it. I feel it has taken me by the hand and*

*is now the final arbiter of my destiny. My fate inextricably*

*linked to and determined by this nether world.*

*So alone I tread through this other world, the collar of my*

*camouflage jacket turned up, my army boots sinking into*

the soft green turf. I smell the strong scent of cordite in the air. Ahead of me, in the distance, flares are flying through the sky like shooting stars. I hear the rumble of heavy artillery and small clouds of smoke drift into the still night air. The sky is illuminated by the weapons of war. I hear the piercing screams of those who have fallen. I feel the pain of those left behind, the mourning of the wives, brothers, fathers, sisters, children and all their loved ones left behind.

I am a soldier, a soldier tired and weary from the many battles of life. Am I not used to apocalyptic scenes? Yet this one is somehow different, like no other battle scene I have witnessed before. I feel as though this world that I now traverse is made up of the fine mesh that divides life from death.

Twilight fades and night takes on her mantle, that deep

black velvet of night, the sanctuary of all life's weary

fighters. In the distance I see the glow of a camp fire. As I

approach, the shadows of the faces of four men are caught

in the red and orange glow as they huddle together around

that eternal fire of comradeship and shared fervor. Those

faces I know, I have seen before in battles long gone. As

Partisans they fought and died and yet they remain

guarding the eternal flames of life.

I continue onwards to witness a scene to two brothers

fighting to the death, like the crusaders, their swords

dancing under the light of the moon, each wearing a

different uniform, yet the blood they spill is the same.

An old woman covered in black garments sits wailing in the

middle of the battlefield. Her eyes are clouded by the signs of advanced glaucoma. Her tears run down the grooves of her face, those grooves etched out by the times of sadness and loss of loved ones. She tells me she is alone, that there is no one left belonging to her, her husband and sons killed in battle, her daughters raped and their throats slits. She asks me who will feed her, who will give her shelter? I have no answers. I continue my journey.

Ahead of me lies a forest, dark and foreboding. I enter this forest and behold a lake. On the edge of this lake sits a monk in saffron robes, his head shaven. He approaches me silently. He puts his hand inside my shirt and rests his fingers on my heart. He withdraws from my heart a bloodied knife and throws it into the lake. I watch as the knife sinks, its covering of dried blood the color of rust is cleansed by the crystal clear waters. He tells me that I can not continue my journey until all the hate is removed from my heart... From there I walk into the depths of the forest where a blind man dressed in rags stumbles along the forest floor; he places his fingers on my face moving them around the contours and with tears in his eyes he tells me he can see what I am feeling.

A deaf woman is sitting under a tree. She is gazing upwards, watching the flight of an owl hunting for its young; she diverts her gaze and stares into my eyes and tells me she can hear what I am thinking.

A white stag stands in front of me and gives me one long piercing look with his deep brown eyes. Two silver tear drops fall onto the forest floor and create two great silver puddles in which I can see my reflection, yet the man I see I *do not recognize. The stag walks away from me; takes one*

*backward glance and then darts away into the forest.*


*I emerge from the forest and as the night moves on so too*

*do I. The far skies show a glimmer of red to herald the*

*approaching dawn. A golden eagle leaves its nest and flies*

*across the rising sun its feathers burnishing gold. A solitary*

*figure wearing a black coat and hood looms in front of me.*

*I see only its profile. It is stationary, unaware of my path*

*that I take. The figure is that of a woman, a beautiful*

*woman. She smiles, her golden curls appear from under*

*her black hood. Her smile is one of comfort, tenderness and*

*understanding. She beckons me to follow her; I do so.*

*By now dawn is upon us as she leads me through lush*

*meadows bestrewn with buttercups. We arrive at the foot*

*of a hill, where the grass is now an emerald green... On top*

*of the hill lie the ruins of a great temple. We climb the hill*

*and arrive at its summit. The temple is without walls. Only*

*the front and rear entrances remain. They are joined*

*together and held in place by one long beam. Along this*

*beam are three sections each containing small altars on*

*which sit religious icons with frankincense burning in front*

*of them.*

*Crowds of people fill the inside and are scattered all*

*around the outside, only a narrow aisle in the center of the*

*temple is free from people. At the end of the aisle is an*

*altar, where earthenware pots full of burning frankincense*

*are place in front of more religious icons. At the altar there*

*are three men and two women facing me as I walk down*

*the aisle; still the lady in the cape leads me on. The people at the front are dressed in long white gowns, indeed the*

*whole congregation is dressed in the same way. Only I*

*remain apart, dressed differently to the others. As I*

*approach the altar the caped lady stands beside me*

*dressed as the others. The faces of those who are now in*

*front of me smile benignly. The edges of their robes are*

*outlined with gold that give off an ethereal shimmering. I*

*am handed a wooden goblet, the kind fashioned by an*

*artisan, I drink deeply and return this sacred chalice.*

*Those in front then lay their hand upon my head and as*

*they do so the congregation closes around me. Then I am*

*gently lifted into the air and carried as if on a coffin pall. I*

*pass the altar and am brought outside the temple to the*

*far end of the hill. I see now that the hill is a cliff. I am*

*carried down a sandy pathway to the sea shore. We enter*

the sea as far up to where the congregations are at waist height in the water. At this point my body is lowered into the sea and my whole body immersed for what seems like an age of time. I am then raised, cleansed by the sea, the faces around me all smiling, lovingly, reassuringly. My clothes are removed and a long white robe is slipped over my neck. I am now part of the congregation.

Along the shore we walk together towards a ship anchored nearby. Her snow white sails are at full billow. The gangway we climb together and soon we are aboard. When the ship is full the anchor is raised and the gangway is drawn back on board. As the ship sails away, we, the congregation, look landwards from where we have come. The great temple and the land soon recede as we start our final journey... I feel a heavenly serenity encompass me. I *turn and look to the horizon on which I see the laughing*

*and dancing eyes of my brother and sister, the silver grey*

*of my mother's hair, the smiles of all my family who have*

*made this journey before me. They are all standing around*

*the olive tree in the desert courtyard of the home where I*

*grew up and was so sublimely happy. Their arms are*

*outstretched. I am now ready to enter my Father's*

*House........ At last I am coming home*

# A LAMENT FOR MIRIAM

**"Suffer little children, and let them come to me, for theirs is the Kingdom of Heaven."   Matthew Chapter 19 verse 14**

Her name was Miriam and she was six years old. She had lustrous raven black hair and jet-black smiling and dancing eyes. Yet it was only when you looked deeply into those eyes that you realized there was something different about Miriam, something special. Miriam was mentally handicapped. She had suffered brain damage at birth. Her mother had had her by caesarian operation and the doctor who had delivered Miriam was poorly trained, and so

*Miriam was doomed to live in a silent world for the rest of her life; she could neither speak nor hear, she could only communicate in the most primitive forms of sign language.*

*Yet despite all this Miriam was happy, very happy and she smiled and laughed a lot. It was clear to all, that those laughs and smiles came right from the depths of her perfect, unblemished soul.*

*Miriam loved life. She loved her Mother and Father, her younger sister, her grandmother, but most of all she loved her new baby brother, Issa, whom she cuddled with great tenderness and affection and in whose company she would be whenever she could. She adored little Issa more than anything in the world.*

She would often play all day with the other children in the village. Those children were also very kind to Miriam, they never taunted nor teased her because in their culture people who were mentally handicapped were said to be "Touched by the hand of God" their place in Paradise was assured as they could not sin, they did not know how, so when they died their passage to heaven was swift and without incumbencies.

So Miriam was happy, probably most of all because she was loved. Her father Yousseff, her mother Fatima, all of her family, and everyone in the desert village of her birth loved her. When she was sick her mother would care and comfort her, when she had nightmares she would crawl into her mother's and father's bed and enjoy that comfort

and protection from fear that can only be gained from the

smell and warmth of your own mother and father. She

would then drop off into a blissful sleep and awake in the

morning with no recall of the fear and demons that had

driven her into her parent's bed the night before.


Miriam wore a small gold chain around her neck on which

was a religious locket that contained a miniaturized

version of The Koran.


One of the things that Miriam liked to do best was to go

with her Mother, Father, sister and baby brother into the

mountains or the desert for a picnic. There she would play

all day with her sister, skipping and dancing and picking

wild flowers. One she would give to her mother, one to her father, and for Issa she would make a garland and place it gently around his neck. Then as dusk approached she would be gathered into her mother's arms where she would fall into a deep sleep, contented and secure with that maternal love instinctively felt by all children held close to the very core and essence of their mother.

She knew about Ramadan, the holy month in her religion, when people would turn their eyes away from the worldly things of life and pass one month in prayer and fasting in grateful thanks to the God who had provided them all with the joys of life.

She also knew that at the end of Ramadan there was a great festival time, called Eid, similar to the Christian Xmas or Easter, a time for celebration and the giving of gifts, Miriam was so excited and looking forward to the coming Eid because she knew that at this time everyone got new clothes. In the local market she had seen this beautiful dress of gold stitch and turquoise silk; her mother had signaled that this would be her gift for Eid and that she would wear this dress on that special day, together with some fine gold braided sandals.

How happy Miriam was. She could see herself, head held proudly, walking through the village, hand in hand with her Mother and Father whilst her friends looked on in admiration at her new Eid dress and all its finery.

Yet in a short space of time her life was to change frantically. The village children were no longer playing in the streets; there was a constant ringing and buzzing in her ears. She saw only great shadows that eclipsed the Moon and the Sun. At first this did not happen too often, but as time passed the eclipses became more frequent. Although Miriam could not hear, she could feel terrible vibrations that racked through her body. She had nightmares more frequently and more often than not at night she would seek the comfort of her parent's bed. You see Miriam had never had never heard of fighter planes or bombing, in fact Miriam had never heard anything at all in her short life.

*The vibrations that racked her body and the ringing in her ears grew with greater intensity as each day passed. She now never left the house and would never stray far from her mother, more often than not clutching at her mother's dress, refusing to release her grip in case she would be swallowed up by the demons who were blacking out the sunlight and giving her terrible headaches. She was so afraid. She did not know what was happening, in her short life she had never experienced anything like this before.*

*No longer was she the happy smiling, laughing child of a few weeks ago. However she thought to herself "Eid "will be here soon and everything will be alright. The sun will shine again, the black demons will disappear. The village children will once again play in the street and of course we will go on our picnics again.*

*Yet this was not to be. One night when the entire village was celebrating a wedding, on of those demons dropped its lethal load on Miriam's village.*

*Through the slanting rays of the sun the following morning the damage was revealed. Miriam lay limp and lifeless like a rag doll, her gold chain and precious locket glinted in the early morning sunlight. Her Mother lay but a few feet away with baby Issa in her arms wrapped in a shawl that was once white but now colored a crimson red, the blood of the mother and child mixed together in death as it had been in birth. The Madonna who had given life to her child*

*and who was there when that life was taken.*

*Never again will Miriam skip and dance through the desert,*

*picking wild flowers with the gentle desert wind blowing*

*through her hair and softly kissing her cheeks. Never again*

*will she hold and cuddle baby Issa. She will not dance*

*through the dusty streets of her desert village on the holy*

*day of Eid, proudly wearing her dress of gold stitch and*

*turquoise and her gold braided sandals. For Miriam is no*

*longer with us. She is in Paradise with her Mother, Father,*

*sister, baby Issa and all those that she loved from the*

*village that no longer is.*

*Miriam was on the American News last night. However she was not called by her own name. She was given another name……. Collateral Damage.*

## DEAD SOULS

*"What passing-bells for these who die as cattle?*

*Only the monstrous anger of guns."*

*"Anthem for doomed youth"*

**Wilfred Owen First World War Poet**

*We have had the order to move out. My Company is patrolling our side of the enemy line. But it is impossible to tell where our line ends and the enemy's begin. There is a great deal of tracer fire, smoke and dust all around. I can't* see anything or anyone. Suddenly I find myself alone, my friends nowhere around me. Its night time and all I can see is a flat expanse of desert and a moonless sky bedecked with thousands of stars. Then I see him. At first he is just a shadow. Then he gets closer. My hands begin to sweat. He is definitely coming towards me. I can not make out his uniform or his face, it is too dark. Is he one of us or is he one of the enemies. I am scared I raise my rifle and release the safety. He is still approaching. He can see me. Still I can not make him out. I raise my rifle and look down the sights. I am beginning to shake. I don't want to kill him unless he is definitely the enemy. I don't want to kill him at all. He is very close now. His outline is clearer. My finger begins to squeeze the trigger. I can see his uniform. He is not one of us. I take aim. I squeeze tighter. He is very close now. I can *make out the outlines of his face. There is something familiar about him. I don't know what. It's not the uniform. Still he is approaching and still his face is becoming more familiar. I squeeze the trigger tighter as his face comes into focus. That face, I am almost sure I know it. He is now closer, I recognize the face, but it is too late. I hear the explosion, feel the recoil, time freezes and the face I am looking at is my own which then explodes into a mass of blood and splintered bone.*

*It is then that I wake up screaming, lying in a pool of cold sweat, shivering and hyperventilating. I don't know where I am. But I know that I have had that same dream again. I have been dreaming the same dream since I arrived here in "Tent City." They call it "Tent City" because that is exactly what it is. A City of tents erected in the desert, both desert and city stretching as far as the eye could see. Row upon row of tents each containing 24 men or women. I doubt whether it has been short listed for any architectural awards, I don't think it was supposed to be. There are no mixed tents but sometimes at night, judging from the sounds made in the bunks, I guess the tents do get a little mixed. But nobody seems to care; nobody seems to care about anything.*

*In the middle of Tent City they have made a recreational center complete with Pizza House and Burger Joints. They have also made a bar. All of these done up in the way they would be done up at home yet the more they try to make it feel like home the more homesick you feel.*

I dig into to my wallet and fish out the photos I carry with me all the time. One of my mum and brothers and sisters. One of my Dad, Granddad and Great Granddad. I look at the two of my grandfather and great grand father. There is definitely a family resemblance, I do look like them. It makes me happy and sad at the same time. My great grand father was killed in The First World War. He was a tunneler, we don't know if the tunnel collapsed or if he was gassed. My grand father killed in Libya in the Second World War. It sends a chill down my spine when I realize that I am the same age now that they were when they died. My dad. Well, my dad, he broke the family mould. In his youth, when he was my age, he was out on the streets on the anti-Vietnam war protests. His whole record collection was full of sixties music, a lot of it anti-war and hippy stuff, you know *"Make Love not war,"* Bob Dylan, Joan Baez, Tom Paxton, Leonard Cohen, Jimi Hendrix, *"Hey man take drugs don't take lives." "Make love, don't make war."*

He wasn't happy about me joining up, he certainly isn't happy about this war. He once said to me when I told him I was going to join the forces *"You don't remember your great grand mother son. I do. I know how she had to struggle to keep the family together after her husband had been killed. They said her husband had died a hero for his country. But that didn't help pay for the food neither did King and country for whom he died. The same goes for my granddad. Of course I don't remember him but I do remember the struggle my grand mum had and the private tears she used to weep in her room when times were hard, clutching in her left hand a handkerchief wiping away her*

*tears while in her right a picture of my grand dad and her*

*on holiday in Bournemouth looking like they both had their*

*whole lives in front of them together, they were happy.  He*

*was dead a year later.*


*I never did see eye to eye with my dad on these matters.*

*We never did get on after I joined up. Yet when I was*

*leaving to come out here he hugged me, I can't remember*

*him ever having done that before. I also thought I saw a*

*tear in his eye as the train pulled out of the station taking*

*me to a RAF (Royal Airforce Base) base to fly out here. He*

*gave me a music tape of John Lennon's. This I have put at*

*the bottom of my knapsack, but I have been listening to it*

*quite a lot recently  Sitting at night in the desert looking at* the stars makes me think a lot more about life and about

my relationship with my dad. Being out here alone in the

desert helps me see and understand things more clearly.

Somehow words seem to mean a lot more out here. I

suppose that's only normal.


"Imagine there's no Heaven,

It's easy if you try,

No Hell below us,

Above us only Sky,

Nothing to kill or die for,

And no religion too,

Imagine all the people living life in peace………"


John Lennon "Imagine."

*I know now that I am beginning to understand and appreciate my dad for the first time in my life. I hope it's not too late. I mean I hope I get to see him again and have a pint with him; we have never really done that before. I have always drunk with my RAF friends. I suppose I was a bit embarrassed about my dad and his politics so I steered clear of his company in the pub. I wonder now if I ever hurt his feelings. He never said anything, but then again he wouldn't. I don't write and tell him what I am thinking, I am a bit embarrassed I suppose. I think if I wrote anything it would sound a bit soppy. Never mind when I get back from here I will definitely have a pint with him and everything will be sorted. I do write to my mum, you know,* the usual stuff "Hi Mum, how's everything, things are great

out here, miss your Sunday Roasts etc........."


It's Saturday evening out here now. The bar is open. Well it

is a huge tent actually. The Padre is one of the barmen,

beaming and smiling, his ruddy face made even ruddier by

the desert sun. There are also three Army girls behind the

bar serving. Everyone is trying to look normal and happy

like they were out drinking in a pub in England. But it

doesn't really work, you know everyone is putting on a face

and probably feeling the same way as I do, afraid and

thinking about their families and what exactly they are

doing out here but nobody says anything. There is this

strange feeling, like this is the last night before we get the order to go to war. People are drinking more and everyone is buying rounds.

All the optics are lined up and most beers are available. There is no draft available, but all cans and bottles that you would find in The U.K. are. Most of the girls are drinking Alco-pops and the guys canned lagers. Outside there is a large tract of desert land made out into a circle. In the space are wooden tables with benches to sit on. You know the kind of seats that you would find in an English Country Pub. But this is like no Country Pub I have ever been to. They have called it "The Queen's Arms" what else! I feel like I am watching a film yet I am also part of it, if you know what I mean. It's difficult to explain it really. But I get the impression everyone feels the same way.

*I walk up to the bar to get the drinks. My mates are outside. There are four of us. We joined up at the same time. We did our training together and have remained mates looking after each other ever since. The Padre comes up smiling benignly, I wonder if they are taught to smile that way when they do their training, you know looking saintly and all that. "Hello Son," he says "How things with you, bearing up are are we?" "Well. I don't know Padre, I mean, do you think its right, and back home most people think that it isn't right. I'm confused, scared I suppose and I keep having these nightmares." He replies, "That's only natural son, you'll be alright, I'll say a prayer for you or if you want you can come to my tent and we will pray together." I look at him, I've heard stories about lads praying with the Padre in his tent and they all say it isn't*

*The Holy Spirit who is trying to come down on you. I smile and take my tray full of drinks outside to my friends.*

*Sean, Johnny and Jimmy are waiting sat around a table." Where have you been Mickey?" they ask. "I was talking with The Padre" I replied "Better be careful with that one" Sean jokes. I nod my head. "Right" says Johnny "Let's drink up and shut up". And so the night continued, round after round, beer after beer, the usual chat, football, sex etc. Yet there was definitely a tension that I hadn't experienced before. After a while the music was turned up. People started dancing. "Look at the body on that one" says Jimmy and so the chat about women continued and the more everyone drank the more people started to dance. There was a feeling of desperation, the kind of desperation* that said to you if you don't do it or get it now you never will, a last chance Motel. My three friends eventually got onto the dance floor. "Come on Micky, or are you waiting for The Padre" they taunted. "No, I'm fine, I'm going to carry on drinking" I replied. I watched all of them, in their desperation trying to forget what lay ahead drinking themselves into the oblivion that would eventually help them slip into a dreamless intoxicated state of sleep.

Next morning at roll call we are told we would be moving out to the front line at nineteen hundred hours. There is an eerie silence after we are dismissed. In fact people are quiet all day, writing letters home, reading, getting kit *together, some of the guys are just staring into space.*

*Everyone is afraid but no one will admit it. Nineteen*

*hundred hours arrived, we are loaded into the armored*

*vehicles and move out to the front. People are sat on*

*benches facing each other but no one says a word. As we*

*get closer to the front we can hear the explosion of artillery*

*shells. I look at my friends sitting opposite me; we smile*

*nervously at each other. I don't think I have ever had better*

*friends in my life before and somehow doubt that I will*

*ever again. There is a peculiar smell in the armored car,*

*like something I have never smelt before; it's getting*

*stronger as we get nearer the front line. I realize then that*

*it is the smell of fear that is almost becoming a stench.*

*We arrive at the front and get out of the armored car. By now the noise of artillery, gun fire is deafening. The soldiers, shouting and screaming, orders are being given, there is a lot of smoke, I can't see anything, every one is confused. Soldiers are running in all directions, bullets whistle by, clouds of smoke, or is it gas, hang in the air, people are falling all around me. I have lost sight of Sean, Johnny and Jimmy. I panic and begin firing blindly. This is madness, the sight is apocalyptic, hell on earth, moaning, piercing shrieks , frenzy abounds, I can't take it anymore, nobody said it would be like this, nobody prepared us, I don't want to die, I am running around aimlessly, tripping over bodies I can't see. Oh God! Suddenly I feel a searing pain rip through the top of my head.*

*I wake up. I am in my bunk, back in tent city. I look around, but the tent is empty. Where is everybody? God that was an awful nightmare. I think I would prefer to have the other. Things are getting to me. Maybe I should see the Doctor and he can give me something to calm me down.*

*I look at my watch, it is 5.30 p.m. How come I have slept for so long? Why didn't anyone wake me? I think to myself I had better check things out. I get dressed. I pull back the flap of the tent and step outside. It is dusk, day quickly fading into night. But that is not all. There is a mist, it comes up to knee level, like an early morning mist that you* would see in England, but I have never seen anything like it out here before. I wade through this swirling mist because my legs feel heavy. I feel like I am wading through a swamp. My heart is beating faster. I feel that there is something not right. But what? I do not know.

Eventually I hear the comforting voice of people as I approach the circular area outside the bar. There seem to be many more tables than before and all of them are full... There is a low murmur of people talking. The kind of sound you would hear from people who were attending a funeral reception.

I walk into the bar and see the back of The Padre. He is filling a glass from one of the optics. I look to see the *reflection of his face in the mirror behind the optic. I gasp;*

*there is no face just a bloody cavity that once held that*

*ruddy leery face. Beside me is a tray of drinks, containing*

*the same drinks as I had bought last night, or was it last*

*night?*

*I walk outside to see my mates sitting at the same table.*

*"Over here Micky" I feel relieved. I saunter over; distribute*

*the drinks without looking up. I sit down and take a long*

*draw of beer and look up smiling. But that smile is soon*

*extinguished. As I look at my mates from left to right I see*

*Sean, his face is all blistered and yellow, he can hardly*

*breathe, and his once big blue eyes have shrunk into the*

*size of small raisins and have gone right onto their sockets.*

*He smiles and as he does so some of his blisters erupt and yellow pus runs down his face.*

*From him I look to Johnny. Johnny takes a long draw of his beer but it all runs down the side of his face, the left side that is, for the right side has been blown away. Thank God Jimmy looks OK; he is drinking and then gets up to shake my hand. As he rises I see the beer pouring out of his stomach. He looks as though he has been disemboweled or fallen on a hand grenade.*

*Is this another nightmare? Out of the corner of my eye I see two men waving in our direction, they are seated at the far end of the circle. They seem to be waving at me. I look towards them and they beckon me over. As I walk through the tables filled with other soldiers I notice people* with horrific battle wounds, limbless torsos with heads rolling around, faceless and half faceless creatures that look less than human, bodies covered with sores, soldiers with their brains and intestines hanging out. I see all kinds of different uniforms that I recognize from bygone wars. Some first world war, second world war, Korean War, Gulf war and many that I do not recognize. Most of the uniforms in Tatters while a few in pristine condition. I make my way through this carnage to the outer perimeter of the circle.

As I get closer to the two men waving at me I think I recognize them. No, this can't be possible, for at the table the men looking at me are the same as those whose photographs are in my wallet. My great Grand father and my Grand father. "Sit down Micky" says the former. I sit and say to them "This can't be real, I must be dreaming because you are both dead." "It is real" he replies "And yes son we are dead," he pauses "And so are you." "No" I scream and bring the back of my right hand to wipe my brow, but there is no brow, there is nothing above my eyes. Realization dawns on me, I too am dead. The top of my head has been blown away. They both look at me Great Grand Father blistered like Sean from gas, Grandfather a gaping hole in his neck from a bayonet charge. "Then I am dead." I hear myself say. "If I am dead, what am I doing here? Oh my god what is going to happen to me? I thought that when you die you go to heaven or hell" I say to them.

*My Great Grand Father looks at me and says in a slow deliberate voice "That is the case for normal people son, but we are not like that. We are soldiers; we have taken the Devil's Shilling. We have broken the Sixth Commandment. "Thou shalt not kill." We have sold our souls. We are doomed to wander this underworld. There is nowhere else for us to go. That is why we are Dead Souls. You are now one of us. Our fate is to travel to every battle that will take place in the future and our numbers will increase. This army of Dead Souls will stalk the underworld until The End of days, The Final Day, Judgment Day. "Then what will happen?" I ask. "Well," he replies "What will happen then, we don't know," he pauses again and after some hesitation he says...... "One can only Imagine."*

## *THE PROPHET*

*High on a mountain top in an isolated region North of Salalah lies the tomb of Job, a Prophet in Judaism, Christianity and Islam. The tomb itself is housed in a small building with a distinctive dome next to a mosque. These two are perched on the edge of the mountainside with breathtaking views down into lush green valleys which lie beneath this mountain range.*

*My journey is to take me to this tomb, a journey which will take three hours by car but which also take me on a journey through a time long gone and a mystical trip through three of the great monotheistic religions.*

*On climbing the mountain road to my destination I take a turning to the right which brings me onto a small twisting lane that leads to the foothills of The Mountains of Qara at*

*the bottom of which flows a natural spring. Coming to the*

*end of the road I am faced with lush green fields on which*

*graze goats, camels and cattle. I get out of my car to*

*breathe in the invigorating air and take some photographs.*

*My attention is drawn to a herd of goats behind which*

*follow an elderly goat herder, dressed in a sarong, tee shirt*

*and a turban and he is carrying an old British Lee Enfield*

*rifle. I greet him in Arabic where upon we engage in a*

*conversation "Where are you from" he asks "From Ireland"*

*I reply, "Oh the same as England" "Not exactly "I say*

*"Maybe it is to the North" he continues, "Yes maybe" I*

*respond. "Where are you going" he continues, "To see the*

*prophet the Tomb of the prophet Job" "You are a Muslim "*

*he replies "No I am a Christian but Job is also a prophet in* our religion" "Ah yes The Bible, I know the book The Bible, it is a good book, we all have the same God." I am struck by the ease and flow of his conversation and his serenity and a sense of his peace and harmony that he finds in his surroundings and his work. His desire to converse on things that are spiritually significant but more than that his obvious inability to divorce his spiritual side from his working life, they are integrated, one, indivisible. There can be no division between them for did not God create everything, himself, the land, his goats and the pastures from which they feed, so how can there be any division. Not at any time am I intimidated by his rifle, in fact as our conversation continues it disappears into my subconscious and our discourse flows as smoothly as the waters from the mountain streams. "What do you do" he asks "I  work with the air force" I reply, his face breaks into a grin "I am

a mere goat herder" he replies and then brings down his

rifle and stands to mock attention and gives me a salute

with a great smile. We both laugh together having

participated in a moment in time of shared communion.

We bid each other farewell wishing upon one another the

blessings of God and he follows his herd onto fresh

pastures and I myself continue onto my own fresh

pastures.


I drive my car back up the lane to the junction and turn

right. The road meanders steeply high into the mountains.

There is no traffic at all, strangely enough I do not expect

any for I feel that for me this is to be a solitary pilgrimage at the end of which I am to learn something of great value

that will sustain and nurture me for the rest of my life.

The appointed time arrives when I come to the Tomb of the

Prophet Job. I pull into the car park where I find myself to

be the lone visitor. There are no other pilgrims, there were

never meant to be.

I get out of my car and feel the stillness and quiet surround

me. It is midday, there is no breeze, I feel the heat of the

sun burning my face. To my left I can smell the pungent,

heady odour of burning frankincense. On turning to my left

I see in the distance a cloud of smoke hanging suspended

just above the line of lush trees that settle beneath the

clear brilliant blue skies that have been borne on the winds

that have arrived from the African Continent. I know

intuitively that this is where the Tomb of Job lies. I walk

*along a path strewn with magnificent bougainvillea in full*

*bloom with blossoms of pink white and orange. I smell the*

*sweet nectar of the Jasmine tree and other exotic perfumes*

*from trees, plants and shrubs that border this twisting*

*pathway whose rock has been smoothed by the passing of*

*time and by the armies of pilgrims who walked this path*

*before me, Kings, Queens, and other pilgrims from the*

*Classical age that is shrouded in the mists of Legends from*

*a time long lost. This shrine visited by so many over such*

*great periods of times is also my destination and I am*

*fated to leave my footprints along with the now ghosts*

*who have trodden this path since the dawn of time. For*

*this place is a mystic site and has always been.*

*As I turn the final bend on the pathway I am confronted by*

*a white edifice, almost square, the size of a normal house,* with a green dome covering the whole roof area. Inside the edifice is the Tomb of Job. There are signs outside, in both English and Arabic asking men to remove their shoes before entering. This I do and then enter the shrine. It is a large room painted white, in the middle of which is the tomb or sarcophagus, no stone or granite is visible for the entire tomb is covered in a green material on which prayers in Arabic are woven into the fabric. There is great serenity to be found here and a profound sense of being somewhere special. The Frankincense is strong and sweet inducing you into an almost trance like state through which you are transcended into another realm where your primeval senses take over your superficial conscious self of the twenty first century.

On leaving the shrine the custodian takes me into the courtyard. This courtyard is an area of scrubland that contains three walls that look as old as time itself, indeed I am to discover that is exactly what they are. The custodian tells me that one of these walls was built to face Jerusalem and that it is from this wall that Job knelt and prayed in the direction of that ancient mystic city. The very city that shares three religions and one God... That being the case why is it that the three religions seem unable to share the one city.

From here I am taken to a small area off the pathway where what looks like a metal trapdoor in the ground lies. The Custodian lifts the trapdoor and as my eyes get accustomed to the dark I can make out a footprint in the rock. I look at the custodian inquisitively and he smiles knowingly at me. "Yes" he says, "This is the footprint of

The Prophet Job." For me it is like The Holy Grail. It is only

then that it becomes clear to me why I have made this

journey. I feel as though the custodian himself knew

beforehand of my arrival. I now see him in a different light;

he appears ethereal, not of this world. His enigmatic smile

continues and there is a shimmering quality to his whole

physical being. "Put your fingers around the outline of the

footprint, feel it, rest your palm on the flat of the foot and

its heel." I gaze at him, startled; for I feel to do something

like this would be tantamount to sacrilege, desecration.

The ethereal messenger reads my thoughts and says "You

must do this thing; it is why you have come to this place."

I lower my hand into this holy place, rest my fingers in the

place where the prints of the toes were and lay the palm of

my hand flat along the length of the foot. I do this carefully, slowly and with a sense of ceremony that embraces my whole being. I feel a sudden surge well up inside me and a strange sensation overcomes me that this footprint and my inner self are forever connected. It is at this exact moment that I realize why I have come and what is to be revealed. It is connected to footprints yet in a figurative way. It is about the life we lead but more importantly the legacy we leave behind after we have departed from this life. Everything we do has a consequence and leaves behind it an effect, whether great or small, and this will leave a residue, a footprint, and this footprint will affect all those around us while we live and those who follow us when we "shed this mortal coil."

We leave behind our footprints and unlike those footprints in the sand these footprints can not be washed away by the winds of time. Like The Footprint of Job, they are forever nwith us. Those we have loved and lost in our souls we carry their footprints. They have not gone from us, how can they when we carry their mark inside our very beings. Like mountain streams they have run their course and have entered The Great Mother Ocean of The Universe. Yet like the dried up river beds they have left their mark for all to see, some more universally evident than others like Moses, Jesus, Mohammed etc. yet still their mark remains within us. Our purpose in life is to leave good, unselfish and meaningful footprints in the souls of others, for them to follow, to comfort them when we depart and when our *river has also run its course and entered The Great Mother*

*Ocean of The Universe.*

*I remove my hand from The Footprint of Job, I look around*

*for the Custodian but I know he will not be there, his task*

*has been completed. I stand up and begin to walk away*

*from the tomb yet I know in my heart and soul I shall never*

*be able to really walk away for my soul will always bear*

*the mark of Job.*

## ARMAGEDDON

**"I beheld a pale horse and him that sat on it was named death, and Hell**

**followed with him."    John "The Book of Revelations."**


So like the opium smokers in the days of Omar Khayyam I

slipped into a deep sleep and my mind drifted beyond the

veil of the night stars and I was taken to a place some

know as "The World of Dreams."

I saw Jesus being crucified on a cross on a hill called

cavalry. I went up to the foot of the cross and looked up

towards him. He gazed down at me and I saw that his

crown of thorns was causing blood to stream down his

face and his tears were also of blood. I asked him "Jesus,

why do you cry tears of blood?" He replied "Look into my

eyes and there you will find the answer." I looked deeply

into his eyes and I saw four horsemen astride large black

menacing stallions. The horsemen were in medieval armor

with a metal visor pulled over their faces so that their

features could not be seen. I saw one of these horsemen

riding through the dusty townships of Africa, his fist raised

in salute, urging people on to slaughter one another, to

hack off limbs, to rape, and I saw him charge by

motherless children standing on street corners wielding AK

47s firing into the air. Another horseman galloped through

the streets of Jerusalem hacking off the heads of women

and children as they walked to worship, I saw blood flow

down the gutters of the alleys where these people lived in

squalor. Yet another carried a plague and drove his horse

through the multitudes of the destitute, the horse blew

thousands of black flies through his nostrils and mouth and covered all those around causing great sickness and death. Orphaned children buried their parents in a world of pestilence, hunger and famine. Children marched on with extended bellies while the dogs of the rich feasted at the table of their masters. Standing on a mountain top in the Land of plenty the fourth horseman watched on as those countries there sold weapons of destruction, sowing the seeds of hatred to those countries whose people are sick and dying and do not have enough to pay for the food nor medicine to treat the sick. I look up at Jesus and ask him why. "They have not understood my message" he says and with that a cloud passes over the sun and the day turns to night. Jesus looks up to the sky and says "My Father why hast thou forsaken me."

## FOR THE ONE I LOST.

**_"I hope that my exit is joyful and I hope never to return."_**

**_Frida Kahlo_**

As I walk through my forest of desolation and loneliness

and arrive in my valley of despair and dejection the wind

rips through my emotions. I ask the wind "On your journey

have you seen the one I have lost?"

The wind fades away and a gentle breeze takes her place

and softly whispers her name and then the one I have lost

is with me. I feel her breath warmly embrace me and my

body tingles with the sense of her presence.

She tells me she is all around me and will always be. She tells me to look into the smiles of small children and in their faces I will see her, to watch the old couple as they sit on the park bench holding hands and in their love I will find her. To gaze at the star filled skies on a clear night and there I will see her smiling.

She tells me that in my darkest moments she will be the candle that will give me light. She tells me that when I wake in the morning she will be waiting for me and that when I leave the house she will be waving to me. She tells me that in my most distressed hour when I can no longer find my direction she will be my compass and will guide me home. She tells me when I feel I can no longer go on and despair fills my soul she will be there to comfort me.

*She tells me never to feel alone for her hands will be*

*forever entwined in mine.*

*She tells me to be happy and live my life and when the time*

*comes her arms will be outstretched and they will be*

*waiting for me.*

## THE SNAKE

Today Salalah is by and large a modern urban sprawl, apart from the Old Souq where you can still walk around the old frankincense market. Indeed Salalah was at one time the centre of The Frankincense Trade and it in this region, that Frankincense, that gold standard of The Ancient World, is grown. It is from here, long ago in an age shrouded in the mists of time, where the caravans of Ancient Worlds started their journeys This was in a time when such figures as The Queen of Sheba ruled The Yemen, the original home of all Arabs, and had palaces and courtiers in Salalah. This is the first place many visitors from all over the world will come. Many Omani women sit cross-legged on the ground in the narrow passageways of the Souq with various bags of frankincense of different quality and different prices. There are usually brightly colored clay frankincense burners and charcoal on sale too in order to fire the frankincense. One of the most fascinating aspects of Salalah is that all around it and outside are archaeological excavations.

On one occasion just after Eid I decided to approach Salalah from another direction east along the coast. This coastal road takes you past rich vegetation, banana trees, coconut trees, and an abundance of other fruits; the sides of the road are a riot of green foliage. At every fifty meters you will find a stall selling coconuts and bananas etc. One has the sensation that one is driving in Africa not Arabia. I stopped at one of these stalls, and an Indian manning the stall, chose a green coconut, and with a machete, hacked away at this fruit, made a small hole in the top, inserted a straw and gave it to me to drink. It was like nectar; I paid the equivalent of fifty pence, got in my car and drove away.

My journey along the coast took me past a large archaeological excavation site that was fenced off.

However there was a gate and a notice board outside. Thinking that this notice board would perhaps give me some information as to the site being excavated I drove my car to the gate and got out to read the notice. The notice gave no information whatsoever regarding the site that was being dug. Rather it was a quotation from the Koran, in both English and Arabic. I shall try to paraphrase its content: "Every creature, be it animal, bird or insect, are all part of God's creation and as such deserve respect from Man, who is God's first creation." I was impressed by the sentiment expressed and drew parallels with other world religions.

I got back into the car and started to drive into the centre of Salalah. Feeling in need of some rest and refreshment I went into a hotel and inquired as to whether there was a coffee shop open. The receptionist led me outside to a great expanse of freshly cut green lawn that backed onto the Indian Ocean where waves of a brilliant blue were crashing onto the shore. Adjacent to the path was a small pile of boulders and as we were approaching I saw the unmistakable shape of a snake slithering into and disappearing down a black hole in this pile of boulders. On my return from the beachside café and arriving at the same pile of boulders I saw the head of the same snake peering around and generally surveying the area. I noticed that the snake had the markings of an Arabian cobra: a highly venomous snake, potentially fatal. The voice of my education said to me "Kill it" so I bent down to pick up a rock and raised my arm to hurl this rock at the snake. Just then my thoughts were drawn back to the notice outside the archaeological site and I realized that this snake was in its home perhaps protecting its young, as any mother would. What right did I have to take this life? I thought again about the sentiments implicit in that quote from the Koran and that if all animals, birds and insects are also part of God's creation, did not God also impart to his animals the same instincts as he passed onto his supreme creation, Man. If so then this snake was acting out of the instinct to protect her young and her home, which perhaps are the two most fundamental instincts that belong to Man, the need for a home and the need to protect and provide for his family. With these thoughts I walked carefully around the snake and back into my car and drove into Salalah where I had some work to do at a bank. Having entered the bank I engaged in conversation with a bank clerk and asked him if he had enjoyed his Eid. "Oh yes," he replied. I then told him I had just seen an Arabian cobra. "Where?" he enquired.

"In the hotel down the road. Perhaps you visited the same one with your family in Eid and the snake was also there at that time."

"Oh no," he replied. "When we are free we spend all our time at home with our family. Life is nothing without a home and a family. A man can own ten thousand camels but without a home, family or love he is a very poor man. Every man needs a home and a family." He continued, "It is not important whether this home is a palace or a hut made from bamboo." I was moved by the simplicity, candor and the priorities of life that were reflected in the sentiment of this casual conversation. Yes, I thought to myself, every creature in God's universe needs a home and it is of no importance whether this home is a grand palace, a small bamboo hut or even a pile of boulders.

As I was driving off home into the blood red sunset I could not help but think how similar the faiths of Judaism, Christianity and Islam are. My mind then went to the peoples of Palestine and Israel. It seemed so clear to me then that the problem there was that simple, each needed a home to call his own and without this there can be no peace or harmony for either of these two peoples. Perhaps we should take more heed of the notice outside the excavation site near Salalah and respect all creatures and their needs, which include man. For if there were mutual respect there would be no wars. Or is it now too late and have the religions and governments of the world been hijacked by those false prophets whom were warned against in The Torah, The Bible and The Koran. For if that is the case "As sure as night follows day" Armageddon too will follow on the heels of these false prophets.

I am reminded of an interview with an old Israeli Lady who was wailing helplessly after an Israeli bus containing school children was blown up. Sobbing she said "When is all this hate and murder going to end. Why can we not learn to love each other and live together? I pray to God for this every night." She then broke down and had to be led away. She had said all that needed to be said.

## THE END

Printed in Great Britain
by Amazon